Picture Recovery

a visual roadmap through the journey of recovery

Mia W. McNary
Artist and Visual Storyteller

Robin G. Simkins
Editor

BEAVER'S
POND
PRESS

PICTURE RECOVERY: A Visual Roadmap Through the Journey of Recovery
© 2022 by Mia W. McNary and Robin G. Simkins

ALCOHOLICS ANONYMOUS® is the registered trademark of Alcoholics Anonymous World Services, Inc., which is not affiliated with and has not endorsed this book.

The author and editor of this book are not medical professionals. The material contained in this book is for informational purposes only and is not a substitute for professional medical advice, diagnosis, or treatment.

Book design and typesetting by James Monroe Design
Production manager: Laurie Buss Herrmann

ISBN 13: 978-1-64343-793-4

Library of Congress Catalog Number: 2021906709

Printed in the United States of America
First Edition: 2022

26 25 24 23 22   5 4 3 2 1

Beaver's Pond Press, Inc.
939 Seventh Street West
Saint Paul, MN 55102
(952) 829-8818
www.BeaversPondPress.com

To order *Picture Recovery* or to set up speaking engagements and interviews, visit www.picturerecoverybook.com.

Find *Picture Recovery* on Facebook and Instagram at PictureRecoveryBook. Tweet *Picture Recovery* at PicRecoveryBook.

To my mom (watching me from above) and dad, for reminding me my whole life how important it is to share my creative gifts with the world.

To my incredible husband, Tim, and our amazing kids, Patrick, Colin, and Mary Jane, for inspiring me to dream big and giving me the creative courage to actually publish this book.

—Mia

To my family. You are where I want to be.

To Mia, for sharing your gifts and enabling my dreams on a global scale.

—Robin

CONTENTS

INTRODUCTION

I started "picturing" recovery to help myself understand the complex issues and remember the many wonderful suggestions I heard at Alcoholics Anonymous meetings. Being a visual learner, like 65 percent of the population, I knew pictures would be key to my recovery and came to rely on them when faced with tough decisions. They were especially critical at the beginning of my sobriety journey, when I had to visually translate *everything*, because to me it all sounded like a foreign language.

Over my twenty-five-plus years in the program, people kept encouraging me to share my pictures, and after much soul-searching, I'm sharing them now in the hopes of helping just one life. If I can be a part of your recovery journey, I'll know this was the right path. Please use this book in whatever way works best for you. It's intended to be a visual roadmap to motivate you to keep going! Carry it with you and take notes or doodle in it to create your own reminders of what you hear during a meeting. Let it be a complement to the following:

- Attending Alcoholics Anonymous meetings
- Calling your sponsor
- Doing service work
- Helping others who are struggling like you
- Staying connected to like-minded people
- Studying the Alcoholics Anonymous literature

We know that people are dying, all around the world, from alcoholism. They are trying to get healthy but feel overwhelmed or even too burned out to read yet another book or to hear yet another piece of advice about achieving sobriety. I frequently left meetings unable to recall what had been said—until I started drawing it. These pictures helped keep my program on track.

I've often said you can't save your face and your ass at the same time. Believing that drinking is still an option, only to realize, once again, that it's not, is humbling. I had to open my mind to find peace, had to risk my own vulnerability, had to draw pictures to help make sense of it all, creating, ultimately, my own personal recovery roadmap. *Picture Recovery* is my offering to you, a visual guide intended to reinforce your decision to remain in the program.

—Mia

Chapter 1
Picture Your Recovery

You are trapped. You don't want to admit it, but you know it. You realize your drinking is out of your control and you need something bigger than yourself to get out.

Losing everything? You're on the verge or have already felt the sting of hitting bottom, probably not for the first time.

You're not doing what you should be doing. When did you realize time was flying? Decide to take action, release defects, and know your full potential!

Can you relate?
A lot of people are living there rent free!
Evict them!

A crazy insane pattern of relapse.

Take stock. What wakes you up?
Have you hit bottom (again)?

ADMIT
COMPLETE
DEFEAT

Does this sound familiar?
Are you worn out and so sad?

Have you lost your focus?

Are you full of self-loathing, and do you keep twisting yourself into a pretzel trying to rationalize your reality?

Do you feel like you have to go into a cave to escape yourself? Are you out of options?

Are you ready to get healthy, whatever it takes?

Your better future is ahead of you. You are ready to believe and to shed the parts of yourself you detest.

Spot new ways to live.

Frozen in time.
Don't ice your reality.

Make an action plan.

Use these visual notes to remember you're not alone and you *can* live to your fullest potential.

Chapter 2
Stop Fighting, You Have a Disease

You need a new map.
A new direction.
You are out of options.

You are ready to SURRENDER your will and listen to others.

Take off the mask.

Learn to admit rather than accept that you are powerless. "Who am I?" Take off the mask!

You have your pride,

but you're not cured of alcoholism.

More is not enough. You know that. Stop debating and realize one drink is too many.

Do you seek out

activities that will get you closer to a drink? Attend concerts? Go to parties?

Are you constantly seeking cover for your drinking?

Do you have a history of relapses? A pattern of trying to stop, only to find yourself with a drink in hand?

Relapse reminds you that **you are powerless** when you believe that drinking is an option. Each person must decide for themselves that they are an alcoholic.

Your ego tells you everything is fine. **You're not fine.** Perhaps you're lacking true, honest reflection? How has your behavior led to the major problems in your life?

Are you **lying** to yourself and others? Deceiving those closest to you?

Still not convinced you are powerless? You make strict rules for how you can drink, only to find yourself back in hot water. Do you often think, "I can stop anytime." Can you? The excuses pile up. You trick yourself and attempt to convince others you're in control.

Overpowering obsession keeps the cycle going. It's a cycle of sick people trying to get well on their own, not of people lacking willpower to stop drinking.

Ask for help.

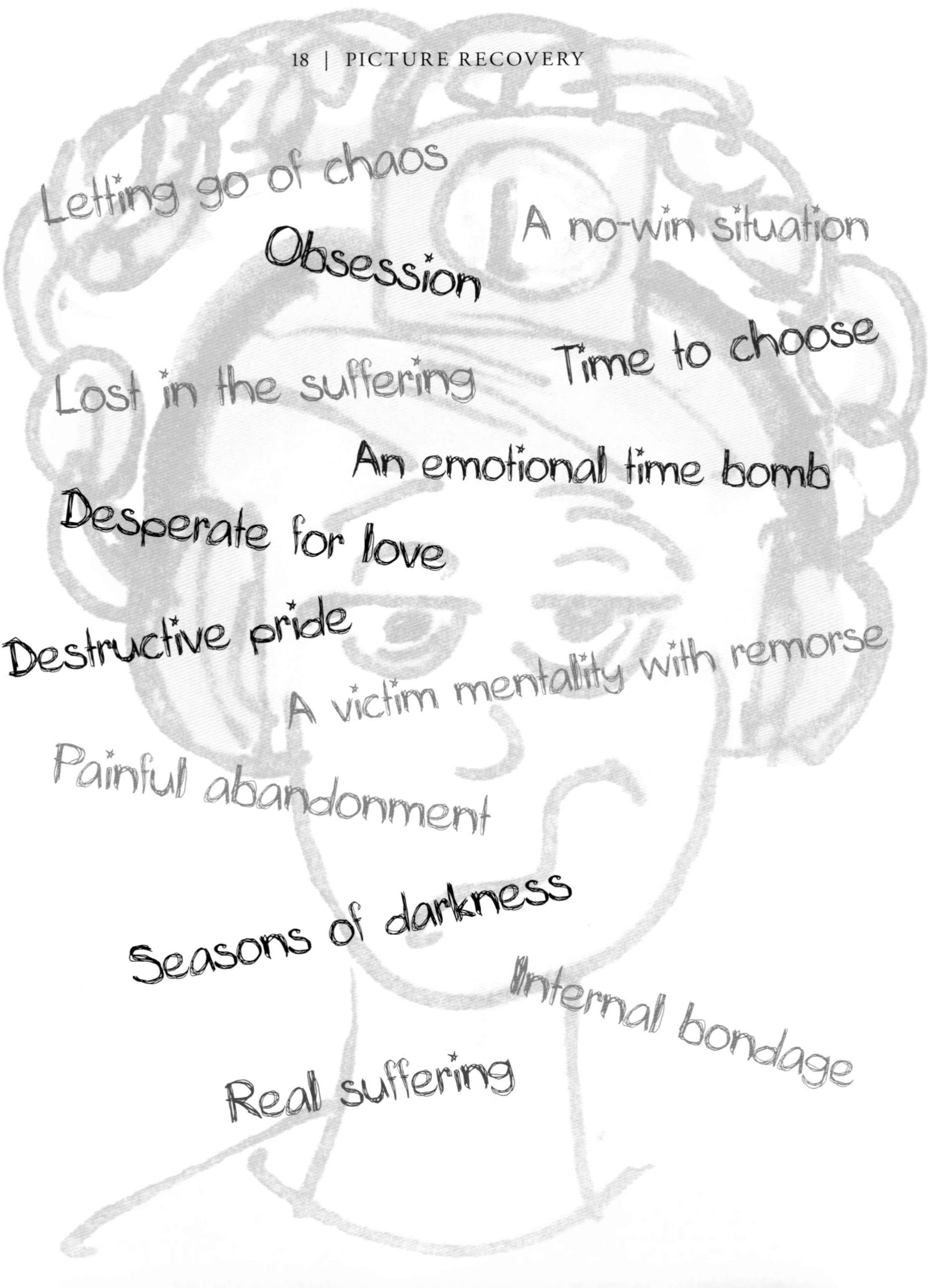

Letting go of chaos

Obsession

A no-win situation

Time to choose

Lost in the suffering

An emotional time bomb

Desperate for love

Destructive pride

A victim mentality with remorse

Painful abandonment

Seasons of darkness

Internal bondage

Real suffering

Chapter 3

Even If It Seems Entirely Foreign, Be Willing to Define Your Higher Power and Practice Being Present Through Meditation or Another Activity

Prayer is especially necessary to the recovery of many, but everyone approaches spirituality with their own biases. Your personal interpretation of, and your belief in, a power greater than yourself is what matters most.

You know you need help. See this opportunity to do life differently.

Pull back the curtain—embrace YOUR understanding of what a higher power is. It's not G-d for everyone.

Sit with space.

Become *aware* of a new source of power.
Stop fighting the war by yourself.

Keep reminding yourself: *My thinking isn't good. I'm not clear. Just because I want something doesn't mean it's right.* Stop yourself from making big changes in your first year of recovery. Do the opposite of what you would normally do.

Pray to a higher power to move you through the process.

The truth will set you free.

Open your heart

to the possibility of help from a higher power.

You're not alone.

This is the end of your isolation.

The alcoholic body has an allergy to alcohol. Alcohol controls the alcoholic! You feel upside-down as you tell people never again, only to have a drink in your hand by the end of the night.

You must find a higher power—anyone other than yourself.

Have vision. Invest in yourself. Strive to reach your full potential. Meditate to rebuild your mind to find clarity in how to live today. Believe in yourself. Remember to choose what's in front of you.

Find pools of blessings

Feel raindrops of truth transformed

Restore hope

Filling the emptiness, you're no longer alone

Dare to believe in your potential

See the video of self—you want a different view

Sick thinking needs a reboot from above

Insanity of life—repeating the
same mistakes over and over

Seek a higher power

Push your powerful secrets into the light (gone)

Take the time to pray and meditate

Chapter 4

Look Inward, Take an Inventory of Past Mistakes, and Share the List with a Trusted Friend

Did you miss out on the promotion at work because you were constantly late?
Take inventory. Examine patterns of your behavior.

Make a list of past events and *reframe* the ways you are powerless over alcohol.

Fill the gaps in your life.

Find new ways.

Keep reading the literature!
Find strength in admitting defeat.

Keep leaning in to receive love and be restored to the best version of yourself.

Release feelings of shame.

Admit you were wrong

Take ownership of
how you harmed others

Face the consequences

Prevent relapses with true wisdom

Avoid the dangerous traps of pride

Escape self-deceptions

Deal with disappointment

Honestly assess the daily journey

Relook at personal boundaries

Squash false images of self

Stop fearing rejection

Right-size your past

Don't look for shortcuts

EMOTIONAL TRAP

Chapter 5

Draw Your Clean Slate with the World and Make Amends to Those You Have Injured, Except When Doing So Would Cause Further Hurt in Their Lives

You have a hole in your heart.

You feel invisible.

You've become part of the background.

Take stock and be seen!

This is your long-awaited-for healing.

Find courage to face the consequences.

Be rid of your emotional sidekicks, "anger" and "fear."

Look for joy.

CLUB OF ANGER

STOP BEATING MYSELF UP

EXIT PLAN

PAUSE BUTTON

Each day presents a new Opportunity to shine a brighter light.

Do your daily cleanup

Make direct confessions

Routinely weed the garden

Feel the nourishment that comes from doing the next right thing

Continue to grow and learn

Dare to experience engagement

Ask for patience, tolerance, kindness, and love as you mend your wrongs

Test the waters for healthier relationships

Breathe in your long-awaited-for healing

Rebuild lost relationships

Be free from shame, fear, and explosive anger

Promises of the program will start to come true

Chapter 6

Take personal stock. Evaluate and reevaluate. Admit when you're wrong, and pledge to do better. Notice goodness!

Stop carrying around your fear and face reality.

You are ready to be honest and to see the happy in everyday happenings.

Use your new tools for coping with anger and tough decisions.

NEW VISION

Release bad patterns.

The road bends.
Keep following the right path.

Don't just talk. Listen!

Embrace new opportunities to learn.

You have a new, solid foundation for facing life.
Stay alert to old patterns and selfish thinking.

Clear away the wreckage of the past

Celebrate your success (a clean slate)

Narrow the road to recovery

See grace

See old patterns and discover healthy paths forward

Have the courage to change

Shift from problem-thinking to problem-solving

Cross the barrier of fear-based thinking

Tell the truth

More is revealed each day of healthy living

Embrace your promised future

SURRENDER

NEGATIVE THOUGHTS

LET IT GO

ACCEPTANCE IS

LIFE STUFF

TODAY ACCEPT PEOPLE PLACES AND EVENTS

TAKE OWNERSHIP ON WRONG-DOING. — CORRECT + MOVE-ON

WHAT IF

WE KNEW

ALL WILL WORK OUT

FLOW OF OUR SOUL

DISCOVER THE BEST OF US

STOP FIGHTIN

STRUGGLE IN ANXIETY

WORRY IS NOT NECESSARY

TRUST H.P.

PUSH BACK DOUBTFUL THINKING

FLYING BY

BLESSINGS

COME

LIFE WILL UNFOLD

WITH FLOW

GOD IS SHOWING ME THE WAY

ACTION MAX. BENEFITS WITH MIN. EFFORT

CONTROL FREAK

LIFE IS EASY

DON'T SWIM UP-STREAM

ACCEPTANCE + GRATITUDE IS ALL YOU NE

NEW WAY

ACCEPT

OLD WAY →

OVER-THINKING

STEP BY STEP NEW SOLUTIONS COME INTO FOCUS

STOP FIGHTING LIFE

MY ACTION MAX TRUS MIN. EFFOR

MASTER CHALLENGE → BY SURRENDERING

OVER-COME BY ACCEPTING-DON'T LABEL IT

Chapter 7
Service Is Key to Finding Your Recovery Life. Help Others Who Need Your Experience, Strength, and Hope. It Feels So Good!

Keep going back to meetings.
Use the support of others in your recovery.

Transmit your knowledge.
You *can* help others.

Connect with people who are doing well in the program.

Group support is important.

It reinforces new behaviors—which is especially important when you're facing
powerful emotions that can arrest recovery.

A shift in your attitude will bring into focus how you can affect the world around you. This shift in behavior and thinking will provide great wisdom for you to share with others who are suffering.

You're qualified to encourage others

This is a gradual miracle—keep waking up

You have a new foundation for facing life

Transform into greatness

Watch out for getting too busy

There's no immunity

Be part of a group

Keep connections with members of your program for stronger insurance

Take a 360-degree approach to your practice

Lend a hand

Stay committed

Be a help

Trust in your ability to teach

SUPER SOBER SELF

Chapter 8
Be the Hero of Your Story

Use your shield to deflect old habits.
Embrace your inner superstar and walk freely in your new life.